*Burn Lyrics* is an entirely original accomplishment. Benjamin Landry has reached into the past and its erasures, and brought into our time and place something new and strange. This collection transforms poetry into lived experience—full of atmosphere and physicality and mysterious specificity and music. Landry is a poet of uncommon gifts, one who has uncovered or discovered an entirely unexpected path for this art form. *Burn Lyrics* began as a remarkable urge, and it is now a spellbinding and transformative reading experience for the rest of us.

LAURA KASISCHKE

Benjamin Landry crafts an eco-lyric voice that celebrates everyday life yet remains "realistic about the future of the coastline." Throughout *Burn Lyrics*, the speaker walks barefoot amongst family and strangers, wolves and goats, hummingbirds and pigeons, greenswards and dandelions, storms and fires. At the end of this journey, the old lyric self sheds its skin and the book becomes a new self to call and return the body home.

CRAIG SANTOS PEREZ

You might think that a poem housing a fragment of sacred text—Sappho's incandescent shards—would be a thing relatively inert in itself: at best a reliquary, at worst a golem. But Benjamin Landry splendidly shatters such preconceptions in this brilliant collection. The landscapes are so captivating, the perspectives so enticing, the emotional currents so swift and strong that you notice, only in passing, that a text you thought long dead has quickened, miraculously, into breathing, exuberant life.

Monica Youn

Benjamin Landry's *Burn Lyrics* both fleshes out the mystery of and satisfies the desires awakened by Sappho's fragments. We are sated at every turn. He is a master not only of the line but also of the heart. Landry offers a new lens through which to view the world; "it's the sort of thing that colors your personal heaven," and, as a reader, I'm left to wonder if this is possible, can the poem curate so much emotion in a world filled with so many distractions, but then I turn another page and realize, "Sometimes, it happens this way."

A. Van Jordan

# Burn Lyrics

Also by Benjamin Landry

*Particle and Wave*

*An Ocean Away*

# Burn Lyrics

Benjamin Landry

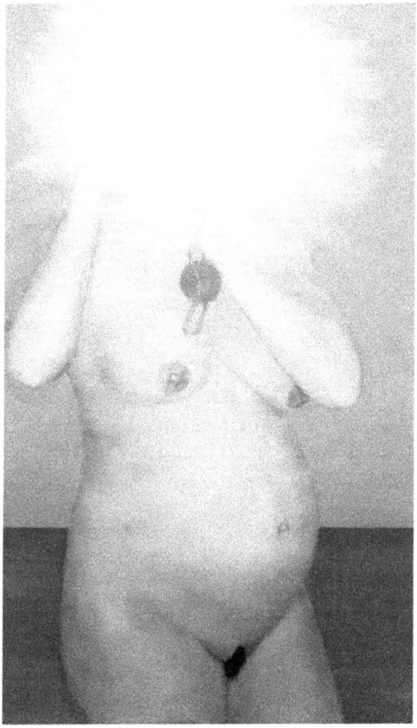

SPUYTEN DUYVIL
*New York City*

Author's Note

I gratefully acknowledge Anne Carson's translation of the extant fragments of Sappho, as rendered in *If Not, Winter*. A list of the fragment sources corresponding to their use in each of my poems is included in the fragment sources note.


ISBN 978-1-941550-95-3



Library of Congress Cataloging-in-Publication Data

Names: Landry, Benjamin, author.
Title: Burn lyrics / Benjamin Landry.
Description: New York City : Spuyten Duyvil, [2016]
Identifiers: LCCN 2015044643 | ISBN 9781941550953 (alk. paper)
Classification: LCC PS3612.A5487 A6 2016 | DDC 811/.6--dc23
LC record available at http://lccn.loc.gov/2015044643

*Sara*

## Contents

I.



II.

III.

IV.

# I.

## In Hudson Valley Light

Just as a thought is an orphan
raised by wolves, just as
a thought is something
barefoot in the Hudson Valley
looking in at squares of light
and the grammar of porcelain.

Just as a thought is balky,
spooked by rapid motion,
aggravated by restraint.
How can it know you mean well?
Put yourself in the place of a thought:
so few kindnesses returned.

# Violet

We're on the bank
like the dead who do not know they're dead

picking out our objective correlatives
from the passing clouds. The day is young.

We still might accomplish a love,
we still might accomplish a translation from the Finnish.

Are we worth our salt? The newest
among us says, "I want to hold

said violet," and the rest of us suspect it won't
work out but don't want to interrupt.

## Patsy Cline

and you
with my longing
you came/burned/cooled
and mind that
I was crazy for you

# You Keep

it is absurd all that time I cowered
in the laurel bush next to the house
trying to think of ways to keep   an early
rufous hummingbird sipped water off
the points of an english oak tree and I
wondered what it would feel like stilled
in the hand   but everything sweeter than
that   and irresistible red for them
o to be an ounce   a traveler unkept
but I scarcely ever listened to their
thrum   it crept up on a soul like
the realization one is not beloved
and keeping seemed such folly now
and the trick was to arrive kindly
like this dynamo that barely touched
down   just as you might have explained
that love had got there first   beautiful
and in the clothes you had laid out for it

## Having

Having come so far, it's difficult
to turn back. You were from
such a treeless town that other
people seemed a heaven,
a wilderness. While they slept,
you wrapped your fingers
in the long, blue grasses
of their lawns. And when
they spoke to you of how you fit
into their ordinary lives, it was
as though they were spreading
a purple cloak over your shoulders.

## What Country?

A bubble you fill in and can't take back:
Choose 'boy.' Choose 'girl.'
The custom of this place seduces;
your wits are restive in the cattle chute,
in a dive bar with a song-long partner
wearing a country dress. We're born

not knowing where we belong.
We learn how to pull knowing grins,
the standard cloth stiff around us.

A storm with your mother's name marches
up the seaboard to the edge of town.
Her warm winds on your ankles make you
yearn for Caribbean places you've never been.

## Raiment

It's a hard fact: the cloth
you wear indicates more
than it conceals. This is
how your adolescence
appeared through broad
sassafras leaves: clever
sateen, impossible damask.
Toothjungles animated
by jasmine dripping.

## Sleepyhead

To the one who comes down
late in the morning, who has managed
to sleep through death
of the old moon. You wear
the transparent mask of the young
and it's a marvel you can align
your eyes with the eyeholes,
your mouth with the lip of the cold coffee cup.

The lawn is dry, the house echoey
with the music you sing in the shower.
Dress slowly, the crescents of your fingers
fitting the buttons on this, the last day
of your old self. Here is a new
one to call your body home.

## Nonbeliever

I don't know
                    move your hand from your mouth
so your 'I don't know' is definite.
        What did he tell Abraham to do?

Like that time your father told
    your brother        *I catch you with pot*
                        *one more time*
*I'll turn you in to*
                                *the police myself.*

What to do?

What to do
                    about the hollow ring
                    of certainty?

I mean, the nine circles of Hell
                    are picturesque,
                    don't get me wrong,
but I can't imagine a kind person

burning because they don't
because they don't
they don't
believe in burning, maybe.

Two states
(sublimated)
of mind in me,

as when your father drives the family
north.  Massachusetts, deciduous,
to New Hampshire, bam, evergreen.

## White-Nose Syndrome

They were of a body,
and their heart grew cold.

By the time the biologist
came to count them,
they had long since
let their wings down.

## Subterraneans

they became like
stars for dark

they stretched
their links
and grew to twice
their normal size

they waved
in the ground
the way something
above was surely
waving in the wind

they quickened
like cells moving
toward a breach

they tried
all the words
they knew to call
the air in

they wondered
who had been
first who would
be left

they became
thoughts of the dead
dreams of grasses

they were
thankful to have
gone unnoticed

they confided
in trilobites
they would
not turn back

they became soft
as they approached
the core

## Stray

I've been accused of many things,
and sure, I most emphatically
came with the privilege of safety,
a home that wanted me. But I
am nobody's sad face, nobody's
nightmare. I'll graze anything:
I'll lie down in the white flowers
and eat the flowers. I am not

someone who likes to give away
the ending. I am not someone
who. I am not someone. I have
exceeded my tender, and how
I wound up over the blue
mountains and away from
the sleeping village is rather
a long story. I tell the circling

wolves *nay*, and it seems to work.
I have a quiet mind.

# II.

## Wild Grape

I am told New Englanders must be distant.

I would like to submit to the court
    of public opinion the sweetest roadside grapes.

I would not presume that everyone
    likes grapes, however sweet.

I would not think that you would
    necessarily get off work at a reasonable
        hour.

I would not think to park on the near
    side of the street; my signal through
        the open window would indicate 'It is I.'

I would not think to touch an ancient
    pack of cigarettes wedged between the seats.

I would not think to touch the radio
    while you crossed to me.

I would not think to touch the sky hanging
    down like a burden of wild grape.

I would not think to touch the sky
with embarrassed laughter, the way
you slump in your seat.

I would not think to touch the sky
with two charged terminals
of our racing poor decisions.
We pull over and stand by the roadside,
gathering, although

I would not think to touch the sky with two arms.

## Stonefruit

Do away with the saccharine
flesh.  It's the heart you will be
interested in, the cyanide pill
one carries through this life.

*That form you loved is*
*absolutely vanished, but*

*I can describe it to you*
*from this side.  It would be*
*for me a pleasure akin*
*to wearing a shark mantle*

*to shine in answer to your*
*blank face as you raise*

one hand having been stained
by the stone's red leach.

## Waiting

years
like packets of sugar
                                        Sweet
'N Low    in sacrifices

as with so many things
                                            having
good shoes makes   a difference

but going to work         feels like
             a rationing of creamer

perverse that from
                           the table
of clerics drifts a discussion
             of miracles
                                        *for we*
*know of works*
             such poor tippers

                           after the dinner
crowd and toward

midnight
the one who waits
to the dark
glass

says *this may be the last time*

## Up Well

Emotion's a strange thing to have
conquered, as though to understand
fear is to master it—a mean
dog—and with delicate words.

It still paces the corridor, slavers past
your woven fingers. This moment's
calm is as translucent as old table cloths
held up to the sun. There's so much

ground to be covered, and the present
taxonomy fails to convince. In short,
it's a scorcher of an afternoon,
and yet her face sleets up well.

## Since Records Have Been Kept

Because greensward
must above
all things drink
the rumor

of fire
crackles through hills.
Aspens quail.  Lindens
shake their golden hair
at the same time.

The West is like an old man
on horseback sick
with this anxiety
of impermanence,
believing storms

should have a faultless
ground.  So greensward
goes on daring,
like faces of youth upraised,

Queen Anne's lace
torchieres touched
to The West you thought
you knew, The West
now a riderless horse.

## Feeling Lucky

Never felt so lucky,
scent of gasoline coming
from the shed, and later,
resurrection lilies bursting
through the tired green.

The rule is we can't
go to sleep feeling lucky.
So, we stay up and talk
about the dawn; how
we may see ourselves
changed. Who wants

to be wise? Lady sings
the blues of whom?
Gold arms of morning
hold us down, and we
wonder if it's the sort
of doom we will outlast.

## At the County Fair

the goatherd is a 4-H-er in fake western regalia
there's popcorn   sawdust in the air   prize longing
klieg lights   hatband sweat   animal lowing   racket
from the tilt-a-whirl   first place is a three hundred
dollar scholarship and a laurel wreath with crimson
roses   what's a goatherd to do but search for love
in the parking lot and the miles of corn beyond that

## Pure Filth

Let's not sing anymore of pigeons
sizing one another up in Washington
Square Park, but I to you

of a white goat tormented by flies
and the rotting fruit just out of reach
on the other side of the slatted fence.

Later, you can describe to me a frieze
in pink sugar, and I will pour wine
over it so that we can enjoy its ruin.

We'll go away like that someday,
all of a sudden, with a burnt, electric
circus smell in the air, it's disgusting.

## Frankenstein's Monster Takes His Bride Aside

Forgive me, love, it sometimes
happens that I can count on only
one hand what I know of you
for certain: you're allergic to mice,
there are some things you cannot
forgive, you're scared of letting
your figure go, you abhor the taste
of celery. It makes me pale to think
of the future we'll have together.
Definitely out of these mountains.

## Vista

The view from here includes the titanium sails
of the greater metropolitan area, an augmented
blue on which it floats, a water wheel
for decorative agraria, grottoes of unchecked
desire, a row of glittering childhood pawnshops,
a whale pod of greensward moving among paths
and tornado sirens. The river—once an industrial
nightmare—smiles at its ingenuity, running
in a cloverleaf. Honeybees make strange,
amplified music. Beholding the vista, one
wonders, *Am I at sea? Am I sleeping on my left side?*
*Am I crazy, or did it seem to me gold chickpeas*
*were growing on the banks?* It is hard to feel
the pleasure of returning home, since the vista
is all places one has been—the haunts—and also
every quarter one is likely to visit. And so, one is
silent with overlapping claustrophobia and awe.

## The Taunting Nobody

It's a terrible thing to ask
how long you've been this way.

To stare into lights is to prefer
the world in a veil of purple

traces. It's too, too
pentecostal, otherwise.

It seems to be the rule
that anyone asked to get

better never does. At least
this way, everyone gets to believe

in a fantasy of their own
making. Like Mary and her

boyfriend with delusions.
What is it you would like to see

today, and with what eyes?

## Messenger

That the cities are on fire
must mean little to you
in your redoubt of spring.

There was a time when
I would wake to your ringtone,
a recording of a nightingale.

If I am with the retinue
of your past, now, insubstantial,
yours is not exactly

a voice of reason,
your indestructible
so-longing.

## To Whitman

chronicler of may lilacs and also of mayhaps   you get tired of ether oysters yellow linen   when you sleep on the recovered battlefield it is with one hand on the breast and the other on the button of your pants   when toward the end you seem carved from a block of stone each fiber of your beard is frost-delicate   reside now in the grass our amazed friend

## Having Left the Window Open

I used to weave crowns
from dandelions [this
is when they were golden
suns and not weeds]. I

used to weave crowns
[from first light stirring
to evening's final flush
of] dandelions. I used

to [give myself to industry;
it was my one ambition
to] weave crowns from
dandelions. I used to

weave [fingers light escaping,
head faulty, unable to distinguish]
crowns from dandelions.
I used to weave

crowns [grave-bright medical
burn, gossip derived, like
a tincture] from dandelions.
I used to weave crowns.

# III.

## Opening Day

Pity is not something that keeps
you warm in a deer stand,

your hands trembling with
cold as the tongues of flame

have been known to tremble,
as the side of the deer,

the flesh beneath
the gold-dusted side

trembles at the stiff
vein of a leaf breaking

in the underbrush.
You're perhaps still accurate;

you're perhaps less so.
By now, you've noticed

old age creeping into
your thoughts. It covers

the ground like sedge,
like new frost. Something

dun and white darts
in the palimpsest

of a canopy. A jet
at thirty thousand feet

flies off in pursuit. If
there's something noble

in this taking—it's hard
for you to say. You'd

rather have that hypothermic
vision, perhaps, of the girl

who used to sing to us,
the one who didn't get

the chance to grow up, the one
with violets in her lap.

Can you remember how the song
goes, how it, in the cracked

air, mostly goes astray?

## Surveilled

Someone is at the window, and it is
not the moonlight.

Something supplies a static
to the telephone connection.

The past will not stand aside and let us
make our own mistakes.

Remember how the acres unspooled,
how you thought you were leaving
to bristle and wave behind?

Now, that fallow swells our temples
and an icy wind compels us
from thought to thought.

What is 'I,' say the even waves
in another room, in another time.

## Necessary Measures

you burn me in effigy

you burn me at the stake

you burn me here and here
to prevent a worse burn from happening

you burn me because
it would be cruel to leave me unburnt

you burn me for your records

you burn me without malice

you burn me where
you wish yourself to be burnt

you burn me for someone else

you burn me to keep in burning practice

you burn me because you were
burnt as a child

you burn me two bricks at a time

you burn me when it is time to eat

you burn me because
you have a match and the wind is right

## Stranger

To please you, I shaved, went to the party, made small talk and mingled with all kinds. I leveraged the vocabulary of success, held my nose and drank Asti. If there was a sunset, I found it marvelous, secretly referring to a clause in my contract. It's the sort of thing that colors your personal heaven. When someone wanted to start a fire, I kneeled to open the flue. When I rose in a full-length mirror, I did not recognize the stranger in the houndstooth coat.

## The Minotaur Keeps It New

The one said to the other,
"I prefer to think of this
as one long game of hide
and seek." Then, the cuckoo
sounded, and the other
pointed to the thick stand
of cedars where the one
would be sought and lost,
and after, left to wonder
where the light had gone
and what the moist,
shuffling breath meant.

## Elegy and Autopsy

—on the eyes, two widely-
circulated coins, too far
tarnished to be 'shiners'

—in the lungs, a pair
of brown monkfish keeping
an ugly silence

—in the mouth, black
and red, a mouth-like
butterfly, wings breathing

—and in the brain, the sleep
of unalloyed night, bedsheets
churning away

## Unemployed

The porch may be a graveyard
for barbecue grills, strollers
and FedEx packages,

but ghosts of suitors still return
to the overhead light
every evening, manyskilled

in persuasion: sharp of dress,
slick of hair, soft of voice,
flowers in a hidden hand.

## When at Last

Sometimes, it happens this way:
one tries to sweep loud enough
to drown out crickets; the other
carries plates to the hutch one
at a time, so as to make more
trips past the window. Two
parts of the life they could have—
in separate dimensions.

Until
a funeral or a storm leaves them
alone together. The air seems
as brittle as one of those plates.
They try to rise from the bed
before they are caught. All night
long, it pulls them back down.

## The Dead Offer Advice

Do
check the weather before leaving the house
enjoy whomever      enjoy however
remember this is how you'll be remembered

Do Not
misplace the faces of anyone
return to the scene of your crime
approach nocturnal animals in daylight

Do Not Move
over warm bodies with onshore fog
your eyes to the right when you lie
toward the light

Do Not Move Stones
from cairns
away from the mouths of caves
from off the chests of us, the dead, unless you
wish to take our place

## Mid-Life

See him up to his wrists in dirt,
feeling for the bulbs he planted. He isn't
scared of dark, wet or sharp. He's been
beestung, and he knows he'll live. It's taken
him half a life to get this way, to get over
the poor impression he made early on
and the friends he always thought he'd see
again who are dead. The sun is high; he can
bear to be alone in the plot that does not
feel under the sky like a water painting
that holds the shape of his thought
for a ghosting moment before it disappears.
He knows there is not time enough left
to get over anything he might lose now.
They'd have to be stored up in the empty
rooms and the attic. The one who survives
is the one who loves indiscriminately,
the one who loves anything new.

# IV.

## Ever Since

the moon broke away from Earth,
it's been trying to woo its way
back. It says, *I've been keeping*
*the universe warm for you;*
*the stars mean nothing to me.*

And the Earth is not indifferent.
See how its waters respond
to each pass, rising like a breast
that wants to believe? Don't we
all believe in love's stupid wisdom?

Don't we believe in makeup sex,
like a bag of black truffles left on
the doorstep in a pale, promising
light of the sort that makes it
so difficult to close one's eyes?

## The Years

Your laughter is
the hammer that breaks
the glass of my reserve.

At times like this, I think
it is possible to fill
a basket with all young sound.

The years say otherwise,
but it is you, only serer
skin, different hair.

## First of the Season

As though forgetting were
discrete, something you could
lead into a dead end, close
the door on. A spotlight

follows you through
your loneliness, follows
you through the frozen
entrée section with your
mental list and gleaming

metal cart. Someone was
singing in the shower: *lyre*
*lyre lyre*. It seems you
had a certain chemistry.

## Art and Architecture

—all those years ago studying
for the exam in Medieval Art and Architecture
in the dimness of the partially shuttered
museum, young men and women—her
classmates, whose names she barely
knew then—cycling before the light
table, staring at the slides quickened
by that brightness—the rounded
flesh tones of Hagia Sophia,
the pinnacles of Mont Saint-Michel.
Their eyes grew tearless; they mouthed
the sacred words of the answers;
they smiled at their exhaustion.

And now, in mid-life, the art
and architecture and the beautiful
strangers have fled her, and her
doctor points to the film on the light box
to a spot whiter by far than an egg.

## Herculaneum

How like a rapture, that
pyroclastic downrushing,
when before there was
the ordinary afternoon:
a dog chasing its tail,
a woman wringing dye
out of cloth, flowers
bowing below a hot cloud
like the breath of a child
about to gather them up.

## Under the Arc

They became unstable,
incandescent.

They became a thing
and its reflection
meeting in the water.

They became two
contradictory thoughts
held in the brain.

They became realistic
about the future
of the coastline.

They became heavier
for wanting.

They became lighter
for not.

## My Darling One

Is it time, already, to put on our shoes
and walk across the bridge? In the other
direction, coyotes lope toward Golden
Gate Park to work on the feral
cat population. We don't acknowledge
one another, maybe because the light
is bad, but maybe something more
fundamental. Is it because our languages
have so thoroughly diverged? Is it
because I imagine you, now, as I have
imagined you all my life, part of my
dying mind? I wanted so much to acquaint
you with a new city, but the skyscrapers
bore you like columns of tears.
Still, it was lovely to watch you
spear that last pimento. I feel I have
gotten that much right, at least.

Fragment Sources Note:

| | |
|---|---|
| In Hudson Valley Light | Fragment 12 |
| Violet | Fragment 76 |
| Patsy Cline | Fragment 48 |
| You Keep | Fragment 62 |
| Having | Fragment 54 |
| What Country? | Fragment 57 |
| Raiment | Fragment 119 |
| Sleepyhead | Fragment 177 |
| Nonbeliever | Fragment 51 |
| White-Nose Syndrome | Fragment 42 |
| Subterraneans | Fragment 61 |
| Stray | Fragment 120 |
| Wild Grape | Fragment 52 |
| Stonefruit | Fragment 4 |
| Waiting | Fragment 19 |
| Up Well | Fragment 100 |
| Since Records Have Been Kept | Fragment 87 |
| Feeling Lucky | Fragment 6 |
| At the County Fair | Fragment 74 |
| Pure Filth | Fragment 40 |
| Frankenstein's Monster Takes His Bride Aside | Fragment 191 |
| Vista | Fragment 143 |
| The Taunting Nobody | Fragment 162 |
| Messenger | Fragment 136 |
| To Whitman | Fragment 126 |
| Having Left the Window Open | Fragment 125 |
| Opening Day | Fragment 21 |
| Surveilled | Fragment 147 |

| | |
|---|---|
| Necessary Measures | Fragment 38 |
| Stranger | Fragment 152 |
| The Minotaur Keeps It New | Fragment 36 |
| Elegy and Autopsy | Fragment 151 |
| Unemployed | Fragment 190 |
| When at Last | Fragment 149 |
| The Dead Offer Advice | Fragment 145 |
| Mid-Life | Fragment 59 |
| Ever Since | Fragment 179 |
| The Years | Fragment 80 |
| First of the Season | Fragment 176 |
| Art and Architecture | Fragment 167 |
| Herculaneum | Fragment 183 |
| Under the Arc | Fragment 61 |
| My Darling One | Fragment 163 |

## Objet Un

what is light  how do we

know it  how does it know us

we are in a boat when

a large bird drops low overhead

and the attendant light

is a green bar in a brown span

that travels down the length

and back again as the angle

fluctuates in relation to the viewer

that green bar like a scanner

understanding by reflection

translating information timely

data need-to-know sending

it somewhere to be housed

the permanent record that

scanning band tipping toward

but never quite reaching

the blunt white end

anomaly of coloration

before tipping back toward

the base quill buried

deep in brute slight body

made for stepping off

into chaos strung

on wires now stalled

killing time as they say

or beyond its consideration

the green bar one star

in a body constellation against

which the viewer is measured

triangulated pressed in cobalt

whitecaps spatterdock

against a granite flank

before which the flinching

faces of lilies like full stops

or placeholders in the permanent

record expand now submerge

to take in the muffled

wedge and cruciform stricken

chrome glimpses above mould

lucent wrack scarlet baubles

long greenish lashes moving

together left right collective

breath shunting the viewer right

left all shifting in relation

to the green bar so that it makes

no sense adds nothing to speak

of name or age irrelevancies

in the permanent record rather

the velocity of living that exceeds

how the green bar halves

then doubles the distance

and never seems to rest

although it must do so

in the blue trajectory of thought

while the viewer serves as weight

and counterweight a line

between endpoints a pick-up

stick a pile of them toward

the laughing far gold-green

arms laden with future pitch

premonitions of rain

transparent net thrown over

the permanent record straining

with this moment always about

to come to fruition as

from the side now the green bar

straight-razors off the tops

of trees punctures the scattered

songbirds' song like that burned

strike the apostrophe

which pretends one thing

belongs to another while

the truth is more tenuous

a series of relations illustrated

physics love for instance

being an occurrence of friction

between creatures as the green

bar returns the quiet rush

to the rushing sound

like something it has dropped

in its haste to be elsewhere

and dust shakes off as it does

along with ice apparent

incendiaries in the tail

of a comet arriving once

every few earth-bound lifetimes

even the green bar flickering
in and out of existence
while it is away this backwater
and its teeming microbia
the soft-bellied things
and the hardened thing
that hunts them moss creeping
out where unexpected
flooded trees subsiding like bone
the hardly-living gray
of scrub oak so that the green

bar passes over them
like a paramedic checking vitals
professional encouraged
the green bar that stands for
there is no inside only outside
and outside the outside
and the holding still that is
an action building imperceptibly
lurking as does the jet
wreathed in stratosphere
sap-drizzled new cones

waiting to brown and fall

the yellow eye in its housing

nails in thorn cornices

blips that make the green bar

quaver recalibrate steady

to horizon and return

to the viewer like a fresh

problem slow faculties nested

layers of fat and nerve and flesh

the indolence of those embodied

heaving on a vast intelligence

the dark amazed brows
unmoored so far from speaking
light years from the shore
as the green bar takes them in
solicitous knees and elbows
bent their young and dying
hands their swanning necks
and ice-bluish eyes
in the pinned moment
they could just begin living
resume breathing if

they could come unpinned

rejoin the red and yellow shapes

through trees the white

and silver on the causeway

what it would mean to them to

come unstuck the green bar

does not record its unmerciful

remembering in the flattened

light past midmorning

beneath a javelin cloud

the air with its faint burnt

odor petals of miniscule flowers
licks of pure color conjured
out of ash leaves of wild
blueberry in ascension hair
and dander spun away on wind all
the cold-blooded things crawled
out bronze-cast to their perches
the veined transparent wings
of insects mid-fan on their bruise-
colored rafts wolf spiders
grappling hungers tuned

to their ledges above
the flash of something lost
each version of this moment
further multiplied as though
they were just the ones
to lay claim although it contains
and escapes them as the green
bar    is it possible    passes
overhead and fades from this
vantage strengthens from another
further down the chain of waters

**Benjamin Landry** is the author of the poetry collections *Particle and Wave* and *An Ocean Away*. He grew up in New England and taught English and creative writing for many years at secondary schools in the United States, Colombia and China, before teaching literature, creative writing and composition at the University of Michigan. He lives in Oberlin, Ohio, with his family—including the fiction writer Sara Schaff—and was a Visiting Assistant Professor of Creative Writing for the fall 2015 term at Oberlin College. His interests include modernism, film, space, memory, visual literacy, dance, fiction and alternative forms. In addition to publishing his poetry widely in journals such as *The Kenyon Review* and *The New Yorker*, he also writes reviews and criticism. Read more about the author at benjaminlandry.wordpress.com.

THUY-VÂN VU (b. Phoenix, AZ) resides in Seattle, WA, and is represented by G. Gibson Gallery. She holds a BFA from the Rhode Island School of Design and an MFA from the University of Texas in Austin. Vu's work largely deals with the mutability of everyday domestic objects, emphasizing their forms by staging them in defamiliarized contexts. Vu's interest in forms of domestic life that have been abstracted from their use continues in her current paintings, which depict museum artifacts. Painting is a way for Vu to re-activate a viewer's experience of objects and places that have been rendered inaccessible. Her paintings relay the tensions that can arise as formal strategies weigh against narratives that may or may not endure.

www.ingramcontent.com/pod-product-compliance
Lightning Source LLC
Chambersburg PA
CBHW020946090426
42736CB00010B/1295
* 9 7 8 1 9 4 1 5 5 0 9 5 3 *